TREES

Ruth Thoms[...]

Designed by Davi[...]
and Nicky Wainwright
Cover design by Josephine Thompson

Illustrated by Bob Bampton,
Wendy Bramall, Paul Brooks,
Frankie Coventry, Sarah Fox-Davies,
Mick Loates, Andy Martin, Dee McLean,
David More, Ralph Stobart, Sally Voke
and James Woods

Edited by Laura Howell
Consultant editor: Esmond Harris B.Sc., Dip.For., F.I.For.
Language consultant: Betty Root

Contents

Amazing facts about trees

Trees are the largest plants in the world. They also live the longest.

On a warm day in spring, a large tree like this takes up enough water from the soil to fill five bathtubs.

Trees cover about one third of the Earth's land surface.

Sometimes, the roots of a tree spread wider than its branches.

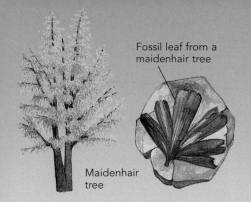

Fossil leaf from a maidenhair tree

Maidenhair tree

Maidenhair trees today look almost the same as the ones that grew 200 million years ago.

Bristlecone pine tree

This type of tree lives for a long time. The oldest one is over 4,750 years old.

This sierra redwood tree grows in California, North America.

People say that this tree has enough wood to make all these buildings. It is the biggest tree in the world. It is 83m (272ft) tall and 24m (79ft) around the trunk.

Go to www.usborne-quicklinks.com for a link to a Web site where you can discover what makes trees and forests so fascinating, and play a match-a-leaf game.

3

Trees in the countryside

This picture shows some of the places where trees grow. Some of them grow naturally and others are planted by people.

This is a windy hillside. The branches of the trees grow bent over because of the wind.

Trees in woods grow close together. They have thin trunks and not very many lower branches.

People sometimes plant trees around their houses to protect them from wind and frost.

A tree growing on its own has spreading branches.

Some trees grow near water.

Go to www.usborne-quicklinks.com for a link to a Web site where you can explore a fantastic forest in an interactive adventure.

Few trees can grow on the hilltops. It is too cold and windy.

Foresters plant pine and spruce trees in straight lines. These trees grow very quickly.

Trees are sometimes planted near roads to give shade.

Every few years, some trees in the forest are cut down. This gives the stronger trees more room to grow.

Trees often mark the edges of fields. They also stop the soil from blowing away.

Under the ground

Roots help a tree in many ways. They take up water and minerals from the soil. A tree needs these things to grow. Roots hold the tree in place and they also hold the soil together. On steep ground, they help stop the soil from washing away in the rain.

Oak tree

Worm

Grubs eat soft, new roots.

The roots are very strong and woody. They help to hold the tree firmly in the ground and stop it from blowing over.

The roots grow a little thicker each year.

Side root

Tap root

Each tree has a main root. This is called the tap root. It grows deep and straight down into the ground.

If a root comes to a stone, it grows around it.

Go to www.usborne-quicklinks.com for a link to a Web site where you can find plant games, activities and information.

Dead leaves fall to the ground. Worms pull them into the soil. The dead leaves contain minerals, which the roots will use again.

Some fungi grow on roots. They help the tree to feed.

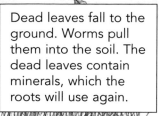

Feeding roots grow from the side roots. They take in water and minerals through their tips. After a few years they die. New roots grow and find fresh soil.

Feeding roots

Side roots grow near the surface of the soil, where there is air and water.

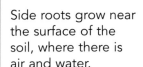

Cockchafer grub

Root tips grow all the time, pushing through the soil. They are covered with hairs, which take in water and minerals.

All roots grow in the direction of water in the soil.

7

How a twig grows

This is how a beech twig grows in one year.

1. Winter

In winter, the bare twigs on the tree begin to grow buds. These will become new stems and leaves.

Leading bud

Side buds

This is the leading bud. It is covered with scales that protect it. The new stem and leaves are inside the scales.

Side shoots

New leaf

The side buds grow into side shoots.

2. Spring

The new stem grows and the leaves unfold. The scales are pushed apart. The new leaves are soft and pale.

Go to **www.usborne-quicklinks.com** for a link to a Web site where you can take a look at a year in the life of a tree, including how its parts grow.

3. Summer

By summer, the stems are stiff and the leaves are dark green and shiny.

New leading bud

4. Autumn

When the twig stops growing, it makes a new leading bud. Next spring, this bud will grow into a new shoot.

The leaves turn brown before they fall off.

New bud

At the end of summer, a new bud is made just above each leaf stalk. Next year, this bud will grow into a new side shoot.

Girdle scar, where leading bud was in winter

The leading bud scales leave a mark called a girdle scar. If you count the girdle scars on a twig, you can find out how old the twig is. This twig is two years old.

Tree stumps

This is the inside of a healthy tree stump. Most of it is sapwood. This carries water and minerals up from the roots to the leaves.

In the middle is heartwood. It is made of old, dead sapwood. It is very hard and strong.

Bark stops the tree from drying out and protects it from insects and disease. Bark cannot stretch. It splits or peels as the wood inside grows. New bark grows underneath.

A new ring of sapwood grows every year.

Sapwood

Heartwood

Bark

Although trees are strong, they may die if fungus attacks them.

Spores

1. Fungus spores in the air get into a wound in the tree.

2. The fungus spreads inside the trunk. The heartwood rots.

The heartwood in this tree is rotten.

3. When the tree gets weak inside, it falls over in a storm.

Go to **www.usborne-quicklinks.com** for a link to a Web site where you can learn more about the different parts of a tree stump.

When a tree dies, the bark becomes loose.
Animals and plants can get under the bark.
Many of them feed on the rotting wood.

Bracket fungi grow on the trunk and feed on the rotting wood.

Slugs eat dead leaves and fungi. In dry weather they hide in cracks under the bark.

Longhorn beetle

Scarlet cup fungi

Bark beetles and their grubs make long tunnels under the bark.

Centipedes live under the bark. They come out at night to hunt for small insects.

Woodlice hide in damp places under the bark. They feed on rotting wood.

Millipedes live on the ground. They feed on dead leaves.

11

Deciduous tree leaves

Many trees are deciduous. This means that they lose their leaves in autumn. Most deciduous trees have soft, flat leaves.

Lime tree

These are lime leaves. Lime trees lose their leaves in autumn.

Rowan

Oak

Vein

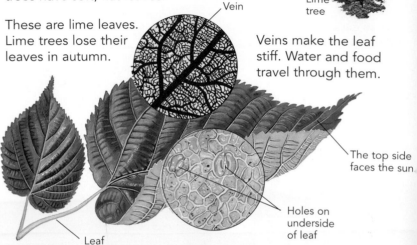

Veins make the leaf stiff. Water and food travel through them.

The top side faces the sun.

Holes on underside of leaf

Leaf stalk

The leaf stalk can bend so that the leaf does not break on windy days. Water and food travel through it.

There are hundreds of tiny holes on the leaf's underside. These open and close to let air in and out and water out.

Sycamore

Quaking aspen

Horse chestnut

Go to www.usborne-quicklinks.com for a link to a Web site where you can find out about a type of evergreen tree called a conifer, with facts and things to do.

Evergreen tree leaves

Trees that keep their leaves all winter are called evergreens. Most evergreens have tough, waxy leaves.

Pine trees have evergreen leaves. Pine leaves are long and narrow. They can stay alive in winter because they are tough and thick. Their waxy skin stops them from drying out. They can still make some food in winter.

Pine leaf

Evergreen leaf veins are in lines.

Italian cypress

Snow gum

Monterey pine

An evergreen tree keeps its leaves for several years. Then they turn brown and fall off. Unlike deciduous trees, they do not fall off all at once. The tree always has some leaves.

Leaves have many different shapes, but they all do the same work. You can find out what they do on the next page.

Norway spruce

Juniper

Evergreen oak

Scots pine

13

What leaves do

A tree breathes and feeds with its leaves. Start at the bottom of the page and follow the numbers to see how a tree makes its food.

3. The leaves take in air.

4. A green chemical in leaves makes food from air and water during the daytime.

2. The water travels up the trunk through tubes in the sapwood.

5. The food moves around the tree in special tubes. These tubes are just under the bark.

Water

Food

1. The roots take up water from the soil.

Go to www.usborne-quicklinks.com for a link to a Web site where you can watch a short animated movie about autumn leaves.

Why do deciduous trees lose their leaves in autumn?

Silver maple

The corky layer forms here.

1. In autumn, it is not warm enough for leaves to make much food. Cold weather would damage soft leaves.

2. A corky layer grows across the leaf stalk. Water cannot get to the leaf any more. The leaf changes shade.

This is a new leaf bud. Below it is the scar where the leaf was joined to the twig.

3. The leaf dries out and dies. The wind blows it off the tree.

4. All the leaves fall off. The tree rests until spring.

Tree flowers

All trees have flowers, even if you don't notice them. Flowers have stamens which hold pollen, and a pistil which holds ovules. Pollen that lands on the top of the pistil grows down to join with the ovules. This is called fertilization. Fertilized ovules grow into seeds.

1. The petals and scent of these flowers attract insects. They feed on a sweet liquid called nectar inside the flower.

This is a stamen. It makes a dust called pollen.

Honey bee

The top of the pistil is called the stigma. Pollen sticks to it.

3. When it visits a flower on another tree, the pollen is brushed onto the stigma. The flower can now make seeds.

2. When an insect comes to feed, it brushes against the stamens. Pollen rubs onto its body.

Go to www.usborne-quicklinks.com for a link to a Web site where you can find a friendly and detailed explanation of what flowers do.

Some trees have two kinds of flowers. One kind has stamens. The other kind has a pistil only. The alder tree on the right has stamen flowers and pistil flowers on the same twig.

Only pistil flowers have ovules and make seeds.

Only stamen flowers make pollen. Lots of them grow together on a long stalk. This is called a catkin.

Catkins come out in the spring before the tree's leaves open. The wind shakes the catkins and the pollen drifts away.

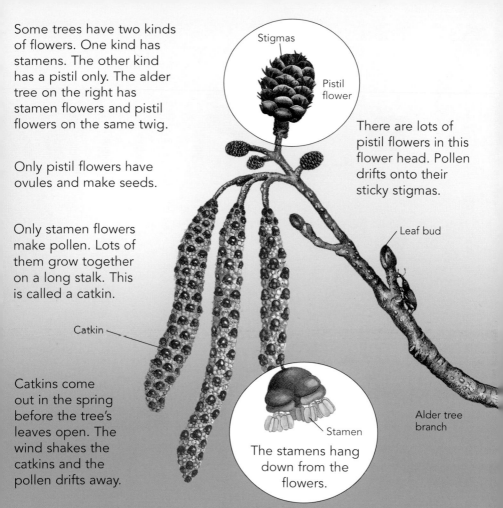

Stigmas

Pistil flower

There are lots of pistil flowers in this flower head. Pollen drifts onto their sticky stigmas.

Leaf bud

Catkin

Stamen

The stamens hang down from the flowers.

Alder tree branch

17

Fruits and seeds

The fertilized ovules grow into seeds. Fruits grow to hold and protect them.

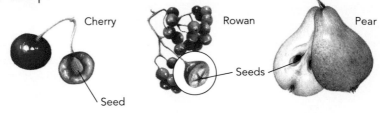

Cherry

Rowan

Pear

Seeds

Seed

These fruits are soft and juicy. Birds and animals eat them. Some have only one seed inside, others have lots.

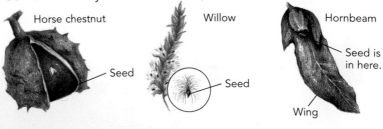

Horse chestnut

Willow

Hornbeam

Seed

Seed

Seed is in here.

Wing

This fruit is spiky. It protects the seed inside.

This fruit is made up of lots of seeds with feathery tops.

This fruit is hard and dry. It has a leafy wing.

Sitka spruce

Lime

Plane

Birch

Beech

Hazel

Go to **www.usborne-quicklinks.com** for a link to a Web site where you can find lots of facts about many different kinds of fruits.

Many evergreen trees have fruits called cones. The flowers that grow at the tips of new shoots grow into cones. Sometimes this takes two years.

Pine flowers are made up of soft scales. Each scale has two ovules inside. When pollen lands on the ovules they start to change into seeds. The scales close up to protect the seeds.

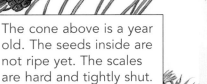

Ovules

A pine flower cut in half

Pine flower

The cone above is a year old. The seeds inside are not ripe yet. The scales are hard and tightly shut.

The cone on the left is two years old. It is large and woody. The seeds inside are ripe. On a dry day, the scales open and the seeds fall out.

Scots pine

Seeds

Yew

Juniper

Crab apple

Mulberry

Sweet chestnut

Black locust

19

How seeds are moved

When the seeds in fruits are ripe, the wind or animals may move them away from the tree. This is because there is not enough light under the parent tree for seedlings to grow well.

Elm

Ash

Sycamore

Fruits with "wings" spin away from the tree.

Falling acorn

Jay

Oak tree

Plane

White poplar

Some fruits are very light. They have tiny hairs that help them float away in the wind.

Squirrels carry acorns away from oak trees and bury them. Birds feed on acorns and drop some. A few of these acorns will grow into trees.

Go to www.usborne-quicklinks.com for a link to a Web site where you can find out how the seeds of some types of trees are moved.

Birds carry the fruits and seeds away from these trees. They eat the fruits and drop the seeds.

Fieldfare

Holly

Blackthorn

Dogwood

Elder

Hawthorn

Waxwing

Alder cone

Seeds

Alder trees grow near water. Their seeds drop in the water and float away. Some seeds will be washed up on a damp river bank. They may grow into new trees.

21

Life in a tree

It's interesting to keep a record book about a tree. Try to see how many insects live on the leaves or rest on the bark. Watch how many birds visit it. Notice if any plants grow on it.

White willow

JUNE

I saw these willow fruits.

JUNE

I found a weevil on a leaf.

When I touched it, it folded its legs.

Some caterpillars are difficult to spot. Search carefully for them.

Herald moth caterpillar

Dragonfly

Flying insects sometimes rest on the leaves of the tree in summer.

Look for willow fruits in spring and summer.

Willow fruits

Poplar hawk moth

This moth is a similar shade to the trunk. It is hard to spot.

Leaf beetle

Look for beetles on the leaves and flowers.

Birds often visit trees to nest or sleep. Some search for seeds or insects.

Red underwing moth

Some moths live on willow trees. They rest in the day and fly away at night.

Index

First published in 2002 by Usborne Publishing Ltd., Usborne House, 83-85 Saffron Hill, London EC1N 8RT, England. **www.usborne.com** Copyright © 2002, 1990, 1982 Usborne Publishing Ltd.